OTHER WORK BY MARC VINCENZ

POETRY

The Propaganda Factory, or Speaking of Trees
Mao's Mole
Gods of a Ransacked Century
Behind the Wall at the Sugar Works (a verse novel)
Beautiful Rush
Additional Breathing Exercises
This Wasted Land and Its Chymical Illuminations
    (annotated by Tom Bradley)
Becoming the Sound of Bees
The Syndicate of Water & Light

LIMITED EDITIONS AND CHAPBOOKS

Benny and the Scottish Blues
Genetic Fires
Upholding Half the Sky
Pull of the Gravitons
Sibylline (illustrated by Dennis Paul Williams)

TRANSLATIONS

Kissing Nests by Werner Lutz
Nightshift / An Area of Shadows by Erika Burkart and Ernst Halter
A Late Recognition of the Signs by Erika Burkart
Grass Grows Inward by Andreas Neeser
Out of the Dust by Klaus Merz
Secret Letter by Erika Burkart
Lifelong Bird Migration by Jürg Amann
Unexpected Development by Klaus Merz
Casting a Spell in Spring by Alexander Xaver Gwerder

FICTION

Three Taos of T'ao, or How to Catch a White Elephant

LEANING
INTO
THE
INFINITE

POEMS

MARC VINCENZ

DOS MADRES

2018

DOS MADRES PRESS INC.

P.O.Box 294, Loveland, Ohio 45140
www.dosmadres.com   editor@dosmadres.com

Dos Madres is dedicated to the belief that the small press is essential
to the vitality of contemporary literature as a carrier of the new voice,
as well as the older, sometimes forgotten voices of the past. And in an
ever more virtual world, to the creation of fine books pleasing to the
eye and hand.

Dos Madres is named in honor of Vera Murphy and Libbie Hughes,
the "Dos Madres" whose contributions have made this press possible.

Dos Madres Press, Inc. is an Ohio Not For Profit Corporation and a
501 (c) (3) qualified public charity. Contributions are tax deductible.

Executive Editor: Robert J. Murphy

Illustration & Book Design: Elizabeth H. Murphy
www.illusionstudios.net
Cover image by Waldemar Borowski

Typeset in Adobe Garamond Pro & Eurostile
ISBN 978-1-948017-00-8
Library of Congress Control Number: 2018933173

First Edition

for Miriam

CONTENTS

ONE
Something Stereophonic Unsettles the Breeze

III. GROSS NATIONAL PRODUCT

IV. SEVEN PRETTY REASONS

V. SOMETHING STEREOPHONIC UNSETTLES THE BREEZE

TWO
Unspeakable Desires

I: IMMEASURABLE CHANGE

II: MYSTIC UTTERANCES

III: THE SLUMBER

IV: SIBYLLINE

ONE

Something Stereophonic Unsettles the Breeze

LISTEN

How a ground
of coffee
may be split

infinitely
to arrive on
different shores.

How a theory
of relativity
may be

written
on a book
of matches.

How the eye
of a moon
may be sipped

in a wine glass
or the face
of a bank-

note may
hold up
a house.

How nothing
is the sound
of itself.

I. PRIMAL INKING

Then nothing will remain of the iron age
And all these people but a thigh-bone or so, a poem
Stuck in the world's thought, splinters of glass
In the rubbish dumps, a concrete dam far off in the mountain …

—Robinson Jeffers, "Summer Holiday"

UNRELIABLE NARRATOR

Should I be
stumped
by the greatness

of God, or—
unlike his
decisions—

should I be
surprised
how arbitrary

these fields of gold
& how they're woven
into a story?

Who then is
the protagonist
when trillions

of single cells
all think
for themselves?—or together?—

Shall I
celebrate
my insig-

nificance
in a 3,000-year-old book?
or should I be

surprised
how a wave
of snow curls

in hesitation, as
if it might be
looking

for an ocean?

CIRCLING THE POLESTAR
AN EMPTY MIND MIRRORS THE WORLD—

Such killing laughter
echoes through

our streets, but who
would want to die

in such tantrically
charged lands?—

Is wild abandon
calling us into

a habitual
moonlight?

Do your thoughts
loop in

& out of
emptiness too?

We tangle together
so well, but how

can we rid
ourselves

of all these damned
abstractions

when the sky is
so immeasurably full?

I know you say: let the mountain
become less

a fuzzy rendering
of ancient calligraphy

but a drunken poet
hunched over

luminous words.

FEW BIRDS SPEAK

Walking home,
the night

is a silent soirée,
& your eyes

squint for light
in the bitter drizzle

as you recall
that dim causeway

on some long-
forgotten holiday

on a tentative moment
at dusk on the Aegean …

Clouds scatter
& the birds hush.

There is no space
to consider

the weather,
when some-

thing stereo-
phonic un-

settles
the breeze.

NUCLEUS

Within the quanta
      the fingerprint
            the spectrum of visibility

Within the orbit
      crossing the line
            of the lifecycle

Within that drowsy sphere
      of what appears to be missing
            surpassing the dreams of the Greeks &—

Within that instant of flux
      a sudden flash
            in the crack

SONG OF ENCHANTMENT

To incant a spell
between the rush

of bodies, a primal urge
to seek out wild frontiers, to go,

flow toe to toe
with the forested bears

& in the singing to sweeten
that background noise.

To delight in coolest mornings
when the lone finch sings

for its mate
from the tree's peak

that it thinks
is a mountain.

To be encountered
in all of this & this, straight

above that noise, in line
of sight with the horizon

& the candlewick burning down
to a low glow.

To unleash everything
that might have been,

a speck of radiation,
a silent overture

to that which never concludes
but rises

& rises

SIXTH DAY OF CREATION: NAGASAKI

Snatched likenesses
from the arts of the senses.

    How else to touch
    a specter.

    Is there really another
surface beneath all this

never-ending smoothness?

When did the gods
that made the neutron

transmute all things
then, give them

        a rippling sense of—

experience?

& why & how with all his wrath,
Pluto struck down

upon that dozy fishing town?

    Souls drained into a lake
    of energy used up—

a small probability which probably
brought us here in the first place.

Was there anything else
in the shuffling

     of the cards, my dove?

HOMO ERECTUS: CINNABAR

They were partly water and partly opaque shape. Fire
desired to arrive in its own image, that's why fire
forced them into flower. They didn't yet have attractive limbs
nor the hand and the lonely voice which fuse in a man.
                                    —Empedocles

In ocher
& hematite

they douse
their hides

seek glory
over stag

& boar &
prairie lion—yet

it is Prometheus
who brings them fire

that cuts
into the heart

of stone &
gives them

the lore
of their love

& the love
of their dominion

11

IN THE ALCHEMY OF A GARDEN

... in Wildness is the preservation of the World.
—Thoreau

Teleological figurines
of a pagan god.

Windbristled, follicled,
fuzzied & furred.

Fantastic fansters
of the brightest illusion,
a luminous love—

O Gold,
heart of an omniscient sun—

a naked moment
of blinded Archimedean recognition

& the *well-well-*
-well of symmetry again—

the meteorology of this simple soil.

& what of her edible symbolism:
a metaphor for all-that-glitters
cross-pollinating with our own?

• • •

In their nefarious dramatis personae,
Odysseus & his crew
bungle on to find Circe,

but the eye is not always sovereign or seen.

This flower garden
is taking on the colors
of human dreams &

the burning desire of every orphan.

ECHOES FROM ANOTHER PLANET

Orpheus: *Prometheus:*

The voice   & what
of time   is that perfume—

becomes audible   that tapdance
finally—   which promises
another time—

within the planes   the word made
of being   Thing

the clip   by the breath
holds the sheaves   of Vayu
together   by the notion

in an abundance   of another world

yet what actually   is as plastic
gives access
to the Thing   as thought itself

Sibyl:

whenever I start
to try & explain it

I forget words
altogether

14

THE BIRTH OF BEAUTY

Weren't things sleepier
before flowers?

Perhaps then they were
the true germ of complex life

which had the power to change
our sense of reality—

that fine line
between poison & desire.

& then arose
those hearty vegetables.

Still more compelling questions
can be answered with jaguar eyes, like:

the meaning of weed & the rain
& that secret wedding of night & fire.

VISION OF CAVE FIRE

At the armchair
of foresight

the strength
of imagination

stereo-
scopic vision

When did we
become we

& burn
the kindling

with our jigsaw
of faculties

postponing
the gratification of desire?

The invention of string?
of the arrow?

Surely the shadow's
flickering magic

is to pierce
a hole

into what
we think

we need
to sow

WAVES DISSOLVE INTO EVENINGS

& ten thousand

        miles

have wandered

        in their wide-eyed tribulations—

from all four corners

        on a curve

only to meet again

        wild

as lovers whirling

        in their maelstrom

cast upon their own

        terra incognita

with angels

        huffing tinted winds

& dragons conjuring

        up another storm

A CYPHER

... for these roses [are] weighted with passion
perfectly and correctly allow themselves
to be decomposed into roses and passion ...
—Roland Barthes

How could they have been defined, when
reaching for a reflection, the mind

was rudely battered by a thrust of ineffable vision?
Where did the book vanish & carry off all the detail?

or, is this the same story even though
it looks quite different on the page.

All that speech made visible, all the sound
contrition of the heart, a confession of deadly sins

& a strange capacity to imagine in order to feel.
Ah, here it lies eroded by slight of tongue, rogue

thoughts as knots on a string, the dead conversing
in bullet points across myopic centuries.

How else could they make a rose bloom again
from its very ashes. Every page may be an oracle

in amorous entanglement—& yet, the first lines
were not songs of love, but checklists of things,

of grain & livestock, of tiles now turned to dust.
Perhaps we should follow the tracks of their creatures

across the pastures to reach the end, or perhaps,
just perhaps, we prefer to be passionately lost.

18

II. FROM A NIMBLE-FINGERED MIND

Or may we say otherwise: that we lived in a golden fleece,
In a rainbow net, in a cloud cocoon
Suspended from the branch of a galactic tree.
And our net was woven from the stuff of signs,
Hieroglyphs for the eye and ear, amorous rings.
A sound reverberated inward, sculpturing our tome,
The flicker, flicker, twitter of our language.

—Czeslaw Milosz "Tidings" (trans. Czeslaw Milosz and Lillian Vallee)

IN THE FLESH

With feet & hands like foreign lands
they pluck their way through space,
encroach not upon themselves
but upon each others' borders
in the flesh, a denouement
tinkling in whiskied ice cubes
almost touching—
that falling-quiet in a fingering
of pauses, then somewhere the shuffle
of Great-grandfather's boots.

For what is a state, says one old man
to another, but a way
of seeing things. & fate,
says the other, deep in his eyebrows,
but a way of seeing things.
It is in the flesh we meet upon
foreign lands, edging closer,
each a fool touching his othermost.

AS COLD & PASSIONATE AS THE DAWN

Here, the will is nothing
more than fading

whispers, a lens
within the lightning

gaze of time,
a misconception—

or that crackling
illusion of fancy footwork

entrenched
in silent woes.

Let me therefore
exhibit a better standing

among this community
of hardy old poets.

THE CURSE OF THE MUMMY

Phantasmagorical cyphers.
Mysteries encoded

in the world's mythologies
may be considered

the metaphysics
of language. Or, perhaps,

to those in the know,
the hieroglyphs

of love's most eager
compulsions.

FROM A NIMBLE-FINGERED MIND

The needle, the awl, the pot
the brazier, the spade, the knot
the bellows, the nail & the screw
the harness, the hook & the shoe
the string, the lever, the loom
the button, the wheel, the silent kaboom

WORD CAUGHT ON THE RIVERBANK

By the river

at night
water carries on

at its own rugged pace

within that

this crooked light
I shall give you

my wildest words

for I shall not

need them
anymore—

you see

even in their sameness

differences
may arouse

a desire

to cast a pebble

& watch it
skim

ad infinitum

when I am dead

you may project me
upon your sunlight

that I may throw

shadows
across your face
& the faces

of those you hold close—

forever

why is that
such a hard word

to catch?

USE OF A DRUM

Orpheus: *Prometheus:*

the delicate   the form
balance   of a wave
of overtones   caught

the halos   in motion, but not
of secondary   action / inter-
meanings   action

the jewel that re-   are not all
flects   ideas rushing
every Other   into the vortex?

of Indra's net   & then—
unimpeded   is the sentence
                                        ever completed?

diminishing

so what then   in the garden
is the language   of earthly desires
Adam spoke
to Eve

                    Sibyl:

                    & where does

                    the sacred fire
                    burn?

above
or
below?

& one last question:

will time come along
& snuff it out?

.

POLYSYLLABIC STEW

A knack, an intuition
to unwind the cables
of mankind in a slow
guttural spread; after
a matter of course, the fuzz
of static becomes not
revelation, but rhetoric—
meanings lost in history
still embedded in the word.

—What we seek, boasts
the oracle in her fancy feathers,
are the sources
of a common culture.

The function
of mnemonics
is memory—to shatter
given fact:
the dialects & dialectics,
the anachronisms & anagrams,
the epithets & all the incantatory
repetitions—
to assimilate assumptions
in mastered oral traditions
still embedded in the word.

THE SATURATED BRILLIANCE
OF THE QUEEN OF THE NIGHT

That year I dragged
spring inside—in winter
they cracked the panes
in their golden veins—

then, the queen, as close
to black as cosmic space
abandoned her sun &
lifted her head to admire

a drunken moon. Imagine
if you will, that bouquet
of deadly sins breathing
through a velvet veil of dark,

imagine her spreading
roots before the thaw
& her dim shadows scattering
across a naked floor.

TRANSCENDENCE

and the gods themselves were nameless, natureless, futureless …
—Enuma Elish

A transfiguration—
new forms before

agricultural revolution
in the everywhen
of a lost paradise:

a tree, a mountain,
a pole, a ladder

embodying the sacred
& profane—before
they are brought down

& that epiphany
of a hidden source

when people wanted
naught from the sky
then, all that wrongdoing

but also the vitality
of a quintessential connection,

the gods of the stratosphere. Did you
not yearn to rise above
where myth & ritual

are embalmed?
Catharsis, Dionysus, bringer

of sweetness toothed, bringer
of light dimmed.
May your sweetness

be the footsteps
of our desire.

How do you blast
your trumpet
with that bumblebee

bouncing off walls?
What a beneficent god!

A liminal figure
bringing wisdom

from the very breast of nature.
& the wine & nectar flow
like flames staring

into the eyes
of a civilization ignited

by the substance of Empire.
& the smoke:
a five-headed century

follows her hot red dust
for two thousand years.

SEEKING A PREGNANT EMPTINESS
ON THE BANKS OF THE RIVER PO

Is this
moonlit-

forest-
moment

the true
seclusion

of a lifetime? &, if so—
the snow

flickering
star-like

the coming &
going

of mystery?—
pray

what prayer
is that?

Some part
of me here

in the now?—
or perhaps

my other self
vanishing

vanishing
back?

III. GROSS NATIONAL PRODUCT

I couldn't face making a merchandise of my mind
—Petrarch

WHEAT UPON A CRESCENT

Tenthousandyearsofharvest
& a hybrid grass believes
man is made for him,

but what of that tower that lies
under forty feet of a crud that civilizes,
the rockbase too a living thing.

Look! You can see it
in the sumptuous thumb-
prints of porticos

         & there!

in the indentations
of ringed toes
winding market stalls, she grows.

& by the way,
did the walls really
tumble down? & in the midst

of all these excavations
did the drum resound
for you?—even just the once?—

Look!
Again.
Thar she blows!

STARGAZERS

The drift
of history

in the under-
tow of legend

in the omens
of portent

& the cycles
of constellations

& the kleptomania
of seers & soothsayers

burning bones
for mystic comfort

& the water music
embracing

the golden apple
in the two-

fold symmetry
of a repeating pattern

where the prop-
erties of space

remain
unbreakable

DISSIPATING CLOUDCOVER

Stormbreak

        distances

unseen

        from the storehouse

lap of rain

        on the shingles

sky

        a downcast brow

waiting

        for a message

waiting

        for a missive

gathering

        in its mystery

APHRODITE & THE FLOOD

Evolution of a city
in perspective—

here in the longest night
windows are eyes.

They flicker half-alive.
Movement & flurries

over tinted rooftops,
then dusk & the painter resumes—

the moment is his fulcrum: drama
in the full face of the model

& the blush of her youth.
Circles whorled into ellipses

traced in empty space
& a kiss. A kiss

on the infant's brow.
Time, of course, is a variable:

the spurt of a plant
in its tangent, the acceleration

upon the slope,
the differential, then

the flux in the infinitesimal.
Such a slow process, to admire

the walls of the citadel
in their own passage

within the sacred
& the sometimes profane—

only this time when she poses
for her portrait, the bust of her

temperament endures
while watching the sun—

what a pastoral scene
cast in shadow, dying

within these four walls,
a symbol of her own

glazed over ice age.
But I ask you this:

despite the migration of birds
& the planets hiding on her face,

how might she predict
the flood & the hurtling of the cannonball?

CROSSING FINGERS, KISSING HANDS

In its shaking,
    its quip & rhyme,
manicured or not,
    the hangnail enshrined.

Crossed, ringed, a rabbit's foot,
    solemn fingers vow
& a hand, the palm knows—
    wipe, swipe, curtsey, bow.

For the divine chanteuse
    where can-can girls tap
in their turning-into
    turning-into magic act—

where sawn in half
    is not the final blow.
Yes, this is no ha'penny
    or dime-store show—

no, not these fingers,
    these tremulous digits
twisting wires on
    knotty trellises. Witness:

where a rose pledges
    thorny allegiance to presidents,
kings whose generous squeezes
    are the rub of a nation's benevolence.

Yes, the hand, the hand,
    the hand's the thing,
that doting underside
    of fatherly loving.

PROMETHEUS'S SPOTTED LIVER

Gibberish brush fire: red earth forget-me-not.

Agent of kinetic change: magic butterknife.

Carver of the unseen written within.

Liberator of the world's innermost essence.

Librarian of nature's innate powers.

Creator of words like *breadfish* & *dovetail*, then—

later: *change, decay, rebirth.*

ECHO

Dark burst
of colors

fills my
eyes &

at land's end
the gate rattles;

fingering
eastern winds,

clouds open
high.

Along this

ragged shore,
a bitter tone:

crows shriek
in lunar ecstasy.

Soft uneven
chains

of melodies
return

as pure
radiance.

A PANTHEON OF LITTLE MERCIES

Seeking
another utopia

wanting to be
the guardians of integrity

& bitter truth
they ignored this

Fearing their idols
they reared the tactics

of bluff & deception
the strategy of better-

the-devil-you-know
the law of averages &

the balance
of opposing impulses

&, in the waiting-to-be-
someone's-illustrious-past

they changed their colors
knowing history was not a chain

of occurrences but a rich feast
of flesh & fallacy

of delicious diatribe
& aromatic dogma

BREAK IN THE BATTLE

Man & unwavering
word in a never-
ending revolution.

To be lost in a forest
with a broken
spear in hand

& that fading
fanatical cackling
echoing across treetops.

The air heavy
with broken bone;
even here, inside,

encircling the fingertips
of pine … In a word,
to carry on,

& finally, in the empty
fucking reaches,
to know it.

SWELL

This person is going to drink you.
Give him a good life
Show him what he wants to know.
                    —Shaman prayer

Seated under the bejeweled tree
of paradise, you murmur to the soil

& the roots—shortly you will begin
your chuckling. It has been said,

when the deceiver is deceived
she will be all the more intoxicating.

You call this your prophetic state,
induced, you say, crosslegged

in lotusknot, by your need for desire;
& in your reclined-head posture

you claim you may breathe more freely
for you have died several times.

Your laughter, therefore, arises
in its greatest potency, above all

when you are engrossed in our woes—
entwined with their larvae & burrowing

beetles. It is here you commune
with you kingdom of fallen feathers

in a single flowering heart.

A LACK OF BLOOD-CERTAINTY

Never again
that chain-reaction
of integrity

O you numbered
obedient ghosts
could well be mistaken

We can it appears
still touch
each other

& in the voice of insurrection
or those birds seen through
the eyes of Velázquez

the seed grows
the hybrid flows
the recessive gene knows

the weight of private thought
being scrutinized
by the Secret Police

then that effervescent coupling
politics buttressed
on a winding staircase

What a totalitarian paradise

To be cloned from Adam's rib
& later, once again, to be revitalized
in a spectacular virgin birth

BREAKING THE SPELL OF MARBLE

Life to the stone by art's free energy …
—Michelangelo

Skeleton
of our city
laid bare
to a storm

& all those practical discoveries

& their well-dressed ideas

Where once terraces wormed

      & waterworks meandered

the wandering curves
      & bends

the busts & torsos & domes & …

          all dead

Just a hand
upon a knee
in the motion
of stone

THE BEGINNINGS OF WISE SILENCE

When thoughts

        begin,

illuminated

        from within:

a canyon,

        a lake,

a valley—

        the mountains

questioning

        the moon—

& at day-

        break,

birds

        in formations

riding

        crests & peaks

with answers

        to everything.

EARLY AUTUMN

Windblown patter
on the mirror
of the lake.

Rippling thoughts
broken
at daybreak.

What else now
but a perfect plume
of smoke?

GROSS NATIONAL PRODUCT

How wrong
our intuition

that objects do not fall
at the same rate:

the oscillation
of odd weights

& their self-determined
downward state.

Thankfully,
the same

cryptic fate
applies to all.

IV. SEVEN PRETTY REASONS

*The reason why seven stars are no more
than seven is a pretty reason.*

—Shakespeare, *King Lear*

STUMBLING POINT

… moments of unageing intellect …
—W.B. Yeats

Figure in the landscape—
more figment than fallacy.

Metabolism bursting
into life; yes, yes:

that up /down (ladders & snakes)
molecular inheritance

—as if we had no past
(were we not so sure of the future)

asserting coherence by fixing
a moment in the crux of the iris,

then tearing it all down
to puzzle it together again:

from the Valley of the River Omo
somewhere near the end

of the beginning, strata
over strata, buried underfoot

& the caracal tracks
or the northward tread

of the oryx, two million
years past; yes, yes:

a leap imagined long
before the leap became itself.

WITHIN A SOURCE OF DESIRE

Rich, dark
lifetime
of after-
noons, one
after an-
other, dying,
cascading, caving into, to-
ward the center of, on
the edge of …

          heavens!
that carnival music—
the hurdy-gurdy
of the carousel, the stuttering
strobe-frame of
the artificial horsemane
or the weathervane cock
yelling *Morning!*—

                  there's the
champagne
but where's the fizz
in the festivity? the
breath
among the clamoring
roses?
in the blur of
the brass band?

—hold on!
in this non-linear sta-
ccatto swoop, cas-
cading, cav-
ing into, to-
ward the center of, on
the edge of ...

an ocean
beneath a crushing sky—
what holy fires burn
in the name of God
on an island ...

IN THE PENAL COLONY

Not from the gagged mouth—it knots & tangles in the larynx
& the chain simply groans: "Have done it.
   Have it etched to the bone."

It's all in the pointed nib of the writers' dark truth.
In an enlightened moment the Bewildered gasps alone—

he knows he is condemned, he shall be bound nude
by his feet, sprung by his neck, stretched from his hands.
   He is bound to intone.

Brushing his bristling tweed the Uniformed flips the switch.
Nobs & spokes gleam: his conscience bears witness to false teeth.

"No doubt, no doubt in guilt, but doubt
  your own compassion," he says.
"When in doubt, doubt blind faith." But then there's another
   voice within—

the sound of an erudite soul chanting praises
  to a virtuous god, the Uniformed
eats his hat, rejoices in the cast iron life ahead, rejoices in the words
   etched on his skin.

How you should love to squelch them beneath your boots like vermin:

Just   **Be**

a
good Citizen

Be   **Just**

&, as the boat leaves the island, you stare at an inner rust
& think: *perhaps it is time to repair the clock.*

BEYOND RECOGNITION

If only I could harvest an epic, & after
the replanting, find the roots of a sophisticated dogma:

I might emerge layered in ash & manure & mud, swerving
to the this-way-that-way of the next light ray.

Could the world come into being again like that?

If only I had a good uncle to sit me down at an uneven hearth
with a hot cup of mulled wine, a twinkle in his eye
& this background whiff of ancient pine:

To hear how the world begins green, fresh, *tabula rasa*:

& late at night or early morning through air still as glass,
to eavesdrop upon the grasses & their endless philosophizing.

THE AUGURIES OF PURE SILENCE

the eternal silence of these infinite spaces frightens me
—Blaise Pascal

Is there a rational explanation
to coax meaning out of a trend
in a constant gravitational field?

Is this the work of a modern world
where each is another's competitor?
What dialogue comes out of that silence?

& who, by Jove, is this prophet anyway?
Is he just a heartening metaphor
for the whims of a heartless emperor?

SKYPOINTERS & GUNCLIMBERS

I have lived with bright stone,
Burned like carnelian in the sun …
                    —Marsden Hartley

Whomever blows
that first kiss
lurches forward
into clouds
of choking smoke
where a young throat
gurgles froth & frost—

& the boys rise
into a tightrope of arms
forming an electric fence
to ward off the burning
through the fingertips
into the palms.
                    & then,

in the middle
of all this heartfelt
conundrum, you coyly ask:
—So lads, as the sun mounts the day,
who is the mother of all this petty crime?

                    —Attend!
                    Attend to your bayonets
                    sweet dogs of youth!

                    —Charge!

VIEW FROM A BACKYARD

A brief metallic sound:
keys upon coins & coins upon keys.
She's saying just do it—&,

it's not acidic like some well-inclined logo
ticked for athletic shoes, at least not
until the afterburn quietens

in the inner view—but there is a problem;
these matches are damp & although
she would love to ignite before the dusk,

she already blazes luminescent, exudes
a whiff of adolescence in her wild spray
of indigo blooms. & I hesitate

to let this cigarette tumble, to witness
all this youth go poof in blinding smoke
that waters. Even these crinkled wrappers

& dented cans smack of romance
in our bold designated light, nuzzling
each other like concerned lovers. Behind

the man-holed chicken wire, torn
from hinges, seething, the defensive
warehouse glares—& from nowhere

a soul sensed, not a single woman pushing
a responsibility, not a lone child spinning
wheels, not even a rat's determined squeak

to disturb this angular indifference. Honestly:
What is the sound of citizens walking
in a new age of supple soles?

V. SOMETHING STEREOPHONIC
UNSETTLES THE BREEZE

ODE TO A METALWORKER
FROM SUMERIAN HEAVEN

(i) Substance & Process

In the laying of the hands
blessing the matter within,

generation over generation at the smith &
the forge at the fire with its ore &

layer over layer hammered
into dented submission—carbonic

for the art of tactic & tantric
for the glory of the empire & the will

of an unruly king & the alchemy
of quenching & the liquid gold

for her splendor, for his self-sacrifice
burning in the bloody heart

of an Aztec sun still to become.

(ii) The Bronze Divine

& malachite fell into the fire
from whence flowed the blood

of the stone, the backbone
of the city cast in her multi-

tude of incorrigible faces.
A paradox that stone-blood

became the heart of man
& with it the tin that was bronze

where the Shang danced upon
the Yellow River & giants flew

to a silver disk of a moon,
& that grand design that illuminates

from her process, the smelter
glowing from that meteorite

that fell, that falls into our hands …

(iii) Element & Action

Ko Hung said, "If it were melted
a hundred times, it should not be spoiled

[with the dross of this world.
Hold the dripping heart of the sun

in your cold, cold fingertips …]."

Mmm, the incorruptible spark
of this human body—& then,

the search for the fire of youth
within the substance & the process,

in the element & the action,
in the sperm becoming embryo,

& stepping through the doors
of secret knowledge into a garden

as children of an egg & a vital fruit.

IN THE MAGNITUDE OF ERRORS

Frowning
into the sun, eyes

see a splinter, no
more than a crack

the rest, un-
knowables

feeding
on the impulse

of fallibility—
chemical compounds

electrifying
engendering

an objective view
to see deeper

into the heart,
to grasp

the ungraspable blood
to feel

the sacred
& profane.

SHORT STROLL

To end

      where

the river

      begins,

not wild

      in anger—no,

lavish

      & rolled up

like & old Persian carpet—

with the last word

      spoken,

&, to be the very last

      to feel

the year's

      uneven

tread.

LAST INDIAN SUMMER

Dawn to dark.

Toil is coming
to an end,

      & water,
that engine of change,

gushes & fans,

a new wave luring
 villagers to the metropolis—

but not without subterfuge
(doesn't social history

creep in from

unexpected places?)—.
It was then they burned

the towns which give rise
to steam

      which fed the iron

& greased the skids;
the sun-god of power

could now be sold
to the everyman

of the everyday, giving

the world its just desserts
in a fixed rate of exchange.

BEDEVILED

In this bee-
happy season

of youth,
saint-like,

across
the wind-

rippled lake,
breathless, you

sub-
merge, but

when cooled
down,

every-
thing

the dawn
dispersed

seizes.

MITOSIS

To have a shape
that repeats forever—

& from foothills
never conquered,

to look
not as you appear

but as you are,
in this uncivilized, arid land

of small crimes—
& where you are

in all of this
wilderness. Everything

else is a matter
of personal suspicion.

THE GOSPEL ACCORDING TO BECKETT

Birth was the death of him.
　　　　　　—Samuel Beckett

To be dead
is not enough, dear—

rather, to be be-
coming

the leaf of a soul
struggling to rustle

into a costume
of earthworms & twigs,

& then to make a home
among the insects

nestled with more
than a holy text

riddled with
unseen difficulties.

How then, my love,
to escape

the circle's vicious
draw?

BODIES THAT SWELL LIKE THE SEA

(i) The Revolution of the Heavenly Orbs

Then that cantankerous quack,
a wick from which the flame
flowed in both dream & knowledge,

that very path those firewalkers tread
bareknuckled in the rain, & thus, eventually
a large number arose within the blanks.

What a body of irrefutable evidence
that lies before us. Did it occur
on Prospero's Island, perhaps?

—for Copernicus

(ii) Unknown in the Elements of Geometry

Behind these Orphic hills, the sea tongues
the lap of hermaphrodite gods who drift
in their smattering of cloud formations,
right-hand-angled in their experience.

But where's the doctrine of proof?
Is it all in the numbers? or within the thymic
hypotenuse?

& thus before matter, there was the invisible.
Was not one hundred oxen sufficient
payment for the gods?
Would not a shake of the hand

have sufficed?
Why then did we need a full embargo?
Yes, yes. It was then those questions
of value arose.

—for Galileo

RADICAL ITCH

In an hour
of the city,

a world
relentlessly

shape-shifts
as clouds sail   westward.

You lie
rumpled

in spice-
stained sheets,

your cheeks
plumpish-pink.

On the street
a car crash.

Two middle-
aged souls

squabble over
left turns

as the umbrella
of gossip puffs out

in dented coffee
cups & on

the monkey bars—
the jarring migraines,

permed, fringed or
feathered, fussing

over diamonds,
choking on pearls,

stuffing symbols
of the future

in well-
lined furls,

weathered
signs of

their long
past-due;

yet that generator
that can never

be fed,
still oozes

oodles
of gluten-

free noodles,
& soon

the night
pounces with stars

& that solitary
uphill tram

wheezes
as crickets sing

folksongs
to the rattle

of upbeat
tambourines,

& cats
scurry home

with life
held tight

between
their teeth.

It's then
you know,

every single dollar
you've ever earned

is as clean
as it's ever

going to be.

IN THE WIDE SPREAD OF HIGH ANTIQUITY

See how curious facts

        form an ungainly wide gait

& press-ganged

        hands wrestle hands

& the demise recorded

        from behind—

Listen to the fading ascent

        nothing but gains

pricked into beauty—

        coins chiming in bones

tantalizing tremors

        & the twisting tongues

See how it creeps up

        in waves & weaves & whistles

        in the inner ear

See how it hides

        between lines

See how easily

        it burns

SURFACE TENSION

Disputed & interspersed. A tactile force
almost, but more: independent, civil, polite—

even strange, as if there were much more
than meets the eye—not a glare, rather

a protracted stare that moves under the skin.

A whiff, a grazing, a chip, a glance—& yet
the nations congregate beneath the seam

of a vivid sky, entwined eye in eye, palm against
palm, tongues poised to call each other artful things.

SUMMER NIGHT IN EARLY SPRING

Naked children
have fallen

asleep under
the tree.

Too late—
the cold world

awakens, rising
out of itself.

At this age
they still know

half their life
belongs to the wild

darkness, & over

their shoulder,
a gentle god.

Ahead lies
a space filled

in with small
kingdoms breathing

needlepoints
of noise. Years

burn. Flesh turns
to stone, but how

does it turn back?

LOVE'S DEATHLESS WOUND

With the heart
from the breasts
of a dozen wily beasts.

With the cluck &
the murmur
the roar & the bleat

& that deep-throated
purring of peculiar
feline pleasures.

With the wit & strength
of elephants swimming
to their secret islands.

With all of this
in full measure
& the good sense
to drink it in.

WHEN A SINGLE SECRET WORLD IS SPOKEN

Finding the Confessor in the Invisible King

The king of pantomime puts it on—he's putting it over
big in the thigh—in his ruffled crepe cuff,
in his chignon eye; nevermind, it will be fine on the night:

I am a shooting star in the real neverneverland.
& in the sound of a thought, waiting for spores
to release from the seat of the soul—

O they're insane for the floodlight.
Now you are a turbulent guest in a memorable fancy—
the Punch & Judy of things past, an object of desire

thumped over the head—& that melting in the air
an instant falling silent as birds in a dark forest, circling
the ceiling for a thousand years to find a good perch …

Each evening after dinner I pour out the wine
for the invisible ones & their furious lives, a music
stretched out across the water, & the spirits

surging through the veins of the mountain, &
those millions of particles filling the capillaries of my heart,
yet off in the distance, the landscape like a line

of ancient Persian script—or perhaps something faintly Japanese?

& when the lightbulb goes out over the all-night city,
I spit out the wind buried in the muscles of my throat.
Jesus, I'm burning for another hot summer, dreaming

of turning back into liquid, to flow where nothing
can be caught out as a symbol of anything else
& drink the blood of broken trees.

THE GREAT MOTHER CONSIDERS HER OWN EMPTINESS & 10,000 SHIMMERING THINGS

Caught in a tirade, Yi says,

even when you fill in
       the emptiness, it remains
emptiness, cosmology &

       language walking hand in hand
(both dead & alive at once);
       10,000 shimmering things

in constant transformation
       & then the emptiness,
the preceding hereafter—

       & before—from
the burgeoning forth
       of spring to the flourish

of summer & the callow
       crawling back into the emptiness
of autumn; but does not

presence arise out of emptiness
       just as language participates
in the rigging of the cosmos

only to reappear in another self, called

Er,

who holds the mandate
        of heaven here on earth,
who begs the question:

        Is there a physical
meta-source
        for ungodly rebirth? Or, perhaps,

San,

who says there are
        always a hundred more:
walls need to be built fast

        to shape the space
for more birth—& who is
        poised for a return

to unscarred simplicity
        slaking a life
in dramatic verse.

SNOWBLINDED

Sailing across the night

            you drop into lost time

                    linger

      on the crust

                    crackle & glare—

caught unaware to find the living

out there

                 beneath a balding moon

on the ice & the snow

                   on the crisp-

sharp-vacuous currents—

                   dead-

     tracked

        red-

           handed

like that black bear with its mouth

full of corn

stumbling upon

a sweet flesh of dawn

creeping

through the maze to greet

the first fluttering of earth

even though you could swear

you once met

before in eyelock—

until

deep into the air you vanish

to settle

a more satisfied planet

Does light move

at the speed of

god?

boundless

in freedom?

all caught

Are we not

TWO

Unspeakable Desires

In the great ceiling of the Sistine Chapel there are readers rather than writers. The prophets and sibyls scrutinize their folios and scrolls. Nothing is written there that we can read. The great pages in their laps and in their hands reflect what happens as if they were mirrors. In front of these blank mirrors the blind prophets are listening. There is only one writer, Jehosaphat the scribe, tucked away in the corner with his scrap of paper, listening to those who really listen.

—Robert Bringhurst, *The Tree of Meaning*

I. IMMEASURABLE CHANGE

WHEN UNCLE FERNANDO CONJURES UP
A DEAD-BIRD THEORY OF EVERYTHING

CHAPTER ONE
In Which Our Dead Bird Speaks of Epic Change in a Foreign Tongue

(i)

In your own myopic view you exist
only as part of your own narrative,
nonplussed by mass & those bundles
of positive energy. Deep in gin, you ask:

Are there really universal truths

when particles become fields & fields, not
underlining, but dragonflying on top of a deadpan description:
symbols based on the metaphor of a bird that dies
in the natural philosophy of its own groundbreaking design?

& with the ice clinking, unpeeling

the layers of this reality shows how restless
you are, even at this hour. For no matter how
silent or how softly something deadly moves,
even a bird squashed on a little-known path to Eden,

is anything truly at rest? & yes,

light is bending toward
all that gravity converging on something
resembling to a straight line. In this billionth
of a second are we just leaves floating

upon an endless Orinoco, Ganges or Amazon?

On the other hand, who cares what occurs
four billion years from now. What is it then
about immortality—that bizarre notion of newness,
the sharp pinch of loose fingers on loose skin

when there really are no words on this page.

       (ii)

& isn't every word mired in what already occurred. Being
is purely a trick of light caught in a blurring
of the here & that visual cortex weaving
in & out of the sky meeting a sea;

& upon its surface two bolts of lightning hurtling.

& didn't we arrive here in a cloud
of toxic gas amidst a whorl of radiation
our collective histories converging
upon something only visible in its own becoming?

You ponder the meaning of all that infinitude.

I have been told the best thing to do
is to stare into the smallest distance, deep
into a zero volume—
for there is no such thing as *needed,*

even in the excesses of a wild imagination.

Several times you've mentioned
your immutable sense of loss
watching those ancient footprints lead away
& how you feel somehow everything

needs to be made up.

UNCLE FERNANDO & SIBYL
EXCHANGE CURT WORDS

Give me
that mythical moment,
he says.

Hush, she says.
Carbon first.
Then light.

AMONG THE NATIVES

—for the Tree God, Saluwaghnapani

(i) Unbroken Eye

O to be born reforested in Borneo

where water doesn't run off in disappointing sloughs,
but cascades & careens within the bejeweled heart
of a single fruiting tree, where a child is a rambutan

(or the fleshy dumpling-pulp of a mangosteen)—

a reflective gleam in its mother's unbroken eye
& the holy spirit hangs cow-low ... for flying foxes
or the Dayak bat wings its eternal-dawn dream

(—through the baritone of echo-you-know

or god-only-knows) (but tell me, what does
a bat god look like?)—in leaf & gnarled bark,
ensnared & entwined in those corkscrew vines

(tenuous binds where pernickety seeds are far-flung)

into an ocean of wild-wielding stillness & into
a window upon that lost-living notion, then simply
shouldering that mutation to the tightly cornered:

(civilization on the salted rim of the home-grown—)

(ii) Dead of Night

Observe, observe the doctor twisting in her smattering
of sunlight, the pensive hammering of her elusive tender fingers,
observe too the rosette of her birthmark flowering

for bees & glorious butterflies, for those pollinators

poised beneath her delicate earlobe—& she, within
the swirling-whir of insect-laden night, listening for
the scrape & scuffle of deadly spiders, the ker-

fuffle of moonrats, or perhaps, perhaps, her nail-

biting companion, a lean South Indian man, now
fervently East American (once turbaned a Sikh, wielding
daggers within his bird's-nest of burdened hair),

tossing in his sleep to the hollow hoot of koels, or the boy

who knows no ladders lying between woman & man,
who was reared on scorpions & snakes & has mastered the art
of the flint-tipped spear, but still recalls

that bedtime rhyme, Milen, his Filipino wet-nurse

claimed drove off demons that grew within Javan
smog clouds: *Ai-Li-Ma-Lu-Ma-Nu* —
& those half-days that sear into weeks &

those moth-eaten weeks that dissolve into dog-

eared months, here amongst the sickly, sticky natives, where a needle
is simply a bandied thread of hope & only he knows
there is no subtle knife to sever those rigid strings.

(iii) A Spell Cast

& within the Clearing of Forbidden Spirits where faces

on poles shrink in arrows of a diminishing sunlight—more
than women or men, a missive to be cutthroat-sold
on a street stall in the City of Gilded Dreams alongside

hand-painted clay pots, baskets woven from native weeds

or insects dried on sticks for a bargain: *Walk No Further.*
You Know This May Be Your Very Last Step. & on that sun
when no midday light rises, when a gold-rimmed stranger

peers from behind the boughs of the Nananuk tree—

they recall the cloudy skies of the plains beyond
where weeds grow tall as trees, he with the obsidian eyes
sneers his knife-edged canines silently, tiger-like,

stalking the gawky kouprey, then raises his palm

as if to the jittery orangutan (who, at any given moment
are poised to flee—forever-deep deep-forever-into the dank,
cavernous interior hiding from any prying predator-senses.)

Tonight the wind weaves.
Tonight the wind whispers & whistles.
Tonight there may be fresh meat.

UNCLE FERNANDO'S DARING ADVICE ON HOW TO ENRICH THE SOIL

Take a strand of language
& forge it in moonlight.

Weave it with artistry &
know in the doing

what really occurred
is more than this:

bury a word or two—
a cherry red noun,

then a dead verb—
for everything you return

shall become part of you:
know then, you are conducting

a holistic pagan rite
steeped in ancient mythology,

watch the emanation
of the numina or the jinn creep

under your tongue & sense
what really occurred

is far-reaching, deep into
the magnetic heart …

for, when shoots emerge
coated in rich sunlight,

your words will become
the skin of the earth.

A STONE A FLINT A KNIFE A SPEAR

(i) Where it has been wrought on cave walls,

reality by inference really. The will of the hand
on the wall anticipates the eyes that shall someday see it—
here at the root whence all knowledge springs—a glance forward
becomes a glance back, & with all that in mind, you ask:

Have you reached the beginning or the end of another ice age?

On the move, she says, civilization can never mature, yet
as the nomad leads her flocks into fragrant pastures,
    the seeds spread far & wide.

&, verily, how the grass may be read in the Sanskrit,
how the grass is the writing on the wall.

(ii) As with the Sibyls,

the flocks are all important, but the she-children constitute a grave
burden. Still, they bake unleavened bread among burning stones
& patiently wait to eat after the infants & grown men.

The milk, the oxen, the yolk & the clotted
yoghurt curdles in their liquid hands—
simplicity is not romantic, they mutter, spit & spin.

Are they are not the weavers & wheelers, the dealers of tales?

A nail, a stirrup, a wooden horse, a bell tolling in the hour of the crow,
no solid features, but with ancient acumen sharpened to a fine point.
& no, not ecclesiastic in the least. They strive when the improbable

may not be traversed & the cross must be burdened but not heard—
old habits survive hard, like Mother's churning, Sister's flourishing
in the sunlight or her dance under a mirrored sky.

They say there are no immortals, simply citizens crossing
themselves year over year, yearning for illimitable time.

UNCLE FERNANDO SUMMONS A STILL WIND

& malarial lands further
south remain still—

not even the grass prickles

& the heady wind pushes off

to embrace her northern shores. Sinking
into the divan, time

seems plush & warm, warmer

still, the Southern Seas

where unthinkable rumors raise
the dead & freedom stinks.

No, no, not a single pigeon coo,

but the night is timid & kind.

Here ministers are ministering—
& in their flurries, geese

arrow off wildly at will;

meanwhile, in my melancholy,

I consult Sibyl what medicine
eases a lifetime

of heart fluttering.

Here we lead a stolen life, she says.
Here the king rounds up men & boys

& all the sensible birds fly due east.

TILT

Shadows—

        fleeting

days—

        sun low

in the west—

        slow

months—

        spiral

of a single

        leaf

all else

        motion-

less—

        just that

noise—

        the years

emptying

CLAMBERING INTO THE ROOTS,

(i) Bats nesting

in tumbleweed hair, clumps
of collagen, furballs—&, in the windpipe,
that intolerable Herculean armhold.

Had she noticed the calm of passersby?
Did she add one pebble to the cairn pile?
Or did she simply watch them grumble & sigh windlike?

Nothing remains, you say?
Just a crumpling of scant evidence.

In this the final glance?
No more, no less?

& what of that three-penny permanence of pyramids?
Or those three-legged lovers racing in their loveknots

prowling halls, gathering the petals
of their loved-me / loved-me-long-forgots?

(ii) Hard facts,

stubbled daylight pincushioning morning.
Weather lost in stone or in a wooden box
or in a hollow bone. & where, near evening,
we get out …

The perfect murder, you say

clambering back into the roots of a home.

The flickering of houselamps reminds me
this is no joke.

UNCLE FERNANDO'S MYTH
OF SACRIFICIAL FIRES

His counter-narrative comes to terms
with meaning-seeking mortality,

then reads in the news: a single foot on the moon
would be a step toward immortality.

To go to a place never seen anywhere
but in the imagined eye of the mind,

then into the heart of great silence
& on to the fetus of rewind—

only here can you be on the other side
so you are a god in your own light.

• • •

Love, an ocean. Rage, a storm.
& the river of sensuality—

the meaning of what occurs,
not what it actually might have been

when something else happens once,
but also all the time.

FERNANDO & SIBYL DWINDLE
IN AN ALTERING LANDSCAPE

Where is this supernatural
intelligence that built
these floundering walls?

the flux of melting colors
& the air ensnared
in its preposterous heat?

Is the folding
of your hands
just a supplication?

As the sun leaves the city
you whisper:

> Do you want me to laugh out loud?

> No. Let us sit here
> you & I—in the darkness,
> old souls knotting fingers

> like once before
> when we were many …
> until that storm of visions

> we concoct
> rises, falls & rips;
> then rips apart again.

LUNAR EFFECT

(I am) shriveled up into such a narrow compass
as is filled by my own bodily sensations …
                                    —Galileo

The middle shifted—

you could barely see it
for all the crowd

    & yet how great

their sublime force
of attraction

    separating in folds

of pure light
they flowered

    in his palm

& wobbled
as he danced

    on his awkward footing—

she took them pressed them
to her lips thinking

    how the stars seemed so far

& then looking across
the flat sea she wondered

    why the world became so narrow

WHEN UNCLE FERNANDO CONJURES UP
A DEAD-BIRD THEORY OF EVERYTHING

CHAPTER TWO
In Which Our Dead Bird Makes a Wretched Discovery

All those weddings held, trumpeting up
speculation on growth & inflation, &
those Saturnalian rings within rings—

A dance of atoms, Sibyl sighs, considering

being or becoming. (*Or, more likely
the fallacy of crooks.) Hand me a smattering
of elixir to cleanse my soul*, she cries.

We negotiate the hours, the fire of expedience,
devouring ourselves in the bones of our knowledge,
both repelled & impelled by that agent
of immeasurable change, the coherence
of figurines that appear to mean something else.

Sibyl quotes Newton: *When bodies
turn to light, light turns into bodies.*

Perhaps this is the most ancient memory
of the first forces of the sun's transmutation,
of the catastrophic ascent

of tribes
of nations
of empires
of civilizations …

ALL THE CREATURES UNDER THE SUN

We see at last the man-faced roe and his
gentle mate; the wild boar too
turns a human face.
            —Robert Duncan, from *Bending the Bow*

Can you still make out the carpenter's plane,
those workboots & that crutch
I leaned upon named Sibyl?

Does the nation fix its thick glass
eye in the mirror? & more strangely, do I feel
the twitch of the sand mite?

Was there was a sea here once?
Now only buildings wobble
in this sickly green land after the highway's end.

Ah, that beginning again
& the rough calcite of slumbering
sea creatures comes off in my hands.

& within the nation's crossflats,
the lichen blots are
stone-draped & dappled.

What pulls us into form then, my dove?
Is it the beaming smile
of that fisheye coming into close focus?

Because, quite haphazardly
on Mondays I swim into the wind
like a particle of sand.

Forgive me, dear Sibyl; perhaps
the time has come.

II. MYSTIC UTTERANCES

There, gracious one, I will place your oracles, and mystic
utterances spoken to my people, and consecrate picked men.
Only do not write your verses on the leaves, lest they fly,
disordered playthings of the rushing winds:
[chart] them from your own mouth.

—Virgil: "The Sibyl's Prophecy," from *The Aeneid, Book VI*

THE SYNDICATE FORESEES
A FAIR DISTRIBUTION OF DOUGH

(i) In the Holy of Holies

6:00 a.m. in the packing department
of *Grandma Jones' Cookie & Cupcake*
factory,

       you cross yourself in imagined
holy water

       even though you can't believe
a single word you just invented—

self-deception is distinctly tart & tannin,

but can't hold a candle to that three-day-old
Sauvignon Blanc Great-auntie Maude
shipped to the aft of her larder,

the only giveaway:
       that awful din,
a clanking in your head
          as the vessel nears
those unmapped rocks.

The gulls still circle your mind.

       (I'll let you guess
       what was rising to the surface.)

& you knew then—counting fingers
in your head—

             all favorable things come
in the better part of three—

even in a rickety state of health
it smells superior to that ornery air
promising all this fulfilling sweetness ...

Sisyphus climbs to the top of the heap.

(ii) An Unrelenting Mind

Extruder number 42 spouts clear
clean polyethylene stamped
in an 80-year-old granny face—

someone someone once adored.

& once again, second shift
       encroaches
upon its dozy third:

   • Ng, Ying Lee (Mrs.)
   • Vietnamese

(whoops, don't index that)—

  &, to the spongy mass of the cupcake gods,
  don't you dare switch off that damn machine
  (even if she badly needs that hip replacement).
  A good company insurance will surely cover it.

She's waggling her doll's head, Ng.

  There's a fine line between legible
  & illegibility, just as the twain doth meet.

You've got her in your sights.
You note, you eye, you lovingly blink

(or was that a wink?).

Remember that fat cheesecake of a man,
you all called Big Joe Marzipan—
he with the nostril hairs you could braid
but didn't dare cross, who walked workshop
floors in squelching rubber boots?—

he would have chopped, quartered & diced,
as he was want to do with pithy fruit—
for all those arched eyebrows,
& for her Asiatic sighs
in their most aromatic spices.

Without you she's dangling—
dangling on a ragged thread,
but you've kindly handed her
that length of sturdy rope to help her bind
what cakes the unrelenting mind …

Oh,—& those smatterings of hope,
                                    religious—almost,

Meanwhile, Mercury in his ankle-wings
loafs about on coupled railings.

BEFORE VAUDEVILLE WAS THE NEXT BIG THING

So—in they slot & plop in their perfectly
burnished, 180-calorie-sandwiched glory:
a delectable mélange well clothed in filigrees

of dietary fibers, sodium, zero trans fat
& generously acidic to keep the heebie-jeebies
at bay—(some, they say, reach as far as Antarctica

in thermal-insulated triple-ply deeply wrought
plastics & other recently uncovered carbon
derivatives—where winds are measured

for incremental fluctuations, where solar flares
are forecast & forewarned, where they read
the beginning & end of stars & the backlash

of East Asian tsunamis)—they glare bright-eyed
in their ginger & chocolate grins, in buttered oatmeal
& butterflied wings—as if finally the Sun reveals

himself in all his shiny glory from behind heady clouds
or that two-week *lune de miel* with its long walks
along the Seine—here, among the boardwalks,

the tulipped promenades, within the boisterous
kite-flying parks that line the fairways, leaves of cypress,
ash, oak & acorn burst in the floppy green of carbon

dioxide, in the piñata emerald of carbon monoxide,
just as Mr. Daniel Ng (also, Ying Lee) glitters starlike
springing in his morning stride to his own *jefe*

at Garcia & Sons, where at midsun he will finally
underwrite Mr. Rujapani's overdue income-tax statement
as starlings, sparrows & blue jays assemble in pecking order

on their own aspen on Pine St. behind the old Empire Theater—
a place once proud to feature *Chang the Magnificent Miracle Man*
or the *Tap-dancing Rubberband Twins*, way back when …

As the giggles of the voluptuous cancan girls
in their petticoats & fishnets echo backstage,
Orpheus returns from the underworld with angel cake.

SIBYL'S SCALES OF JUSTICE

Her eternal return:

feathered, cloaked in stars, hollowed out
from the ether, washed up
from the seven seas—she will.

& sifted from the dirt, scraped
from the inside of a stormcloud, she bears
her lightning rods, her scales

& her flaming shield. With her dragonfly wings
she hovers, & in her golden talons &
something resembling a coiled rope—

this as certain as the ant
crushed carelessly under the weight
of your soul.

Once day, I will ask her:

Are we not all one & alone,
& the same
one-alone at that?

There cannot just be the one
chance though, can there?
For surely there is none in paradise.

Over there, are not all things
created in one blinding flash
of insight?

UNCLE FERNANDO LEARNS TO TURN
THE HURDY-GURDY

Again, venturing forth, the mariner becomes peacefully landlocked

In ancient China,
to snatch the moon
from the sky
was *to live.*

          The forces
that produce the oak lie potent
within the acorn—

months & years tighten &
push each other away
to make room for that dull silence
of forgotten desires.

Don't you want to set out
on a journey & never look back?

In a moment of solitude on Monte Alban, 1984

Do you see
your way through
these melting
mountain peaks?

Keep your ears cocked
to the wind,

for when tomorrow
finally arrives,
it never seems
like tomorrow.

        Finally, at the top,
looking across quilts of snow
a spirit blindly fumbles,
chasing her own tail, until—

she sees me, brakes
into dance, whirls,
then chases herself away.

THE TRUE TIMELINE OF AN OLD MAGICK MAN

Whiskeyvoiced &
honeysuckled, an
heirloom prancing

pillar to post, &
cupid surreptitiously
wingless, a marvelous-

marsupial-tree-climbing-
nut (he hoodwinked her
hoping she would shoot)—

sequinned & squinting &
sloshing over, then that
deliciously warm tickle
in his throat. As the water fans

the river wheel & the stones
heat up in the sun & the trees
sway in a lasting forgiveness, she sighs:

"No more stars, please, Fernando.
Let us live willfully
close to our ghosts."

TWO POEMS FOR SWEET SIBYL

There is always sufficient
Reason for a horror of
The use of the pronoun "I".
   —Kenneth Rexroth, "Codicil"

Consumed with Her Specters

In those sickening days
she reaches out, then
clears her throat
for a single
slant-rhyme.

That Passionate High

Within that first summer,
a sumptuous smile. & then,
unquestioningly,
that fabulous apparition
coins herself.

UNCLE FERNANDO'S ADVICE ON
FLYAWAY HAIR

Have you taken note
of the drift
of your own South Sea Islands?

Have you considered how long
they've held their heads
above the bruised coral reefs?

& how long will
the manta ray
cast winged shadows?

& do not forget those lonely fishermen
with their whitebait & tin traps
opening the can over & over until

they have only scraps & scrapings, ink &
paper on calluses, or depth charges
that run wild where continental plates collide.

Do the ghosts of their catches circle your boats
in shoals as the gulls circling the city root deep
in the landfill of another bygone era?

Take note.
Observe everything.
One bird at a time.

WHEN UNCLE FERNANDO CONJURES UP
A DEAD-BIRD THEORY OF EVERYTHING

CHAPTER THREE
In Which Our Dead Bird Notices an Erroneous Light Rising

In the biopic of the now
(which doesn't truly exist
as we've previously established, yes?)
what is water & what is light?—

both neither particle nor wave?

by like forces that agent
an immeasurable change,
the coherence of the figures that appear—
it's all about context you've said.

Nothing remains what it is

for very long, & yet, is not
our own quantum state subtle,
negligible, bacterial—spectral
fingerprints in a haze of dualities,

the perfection of the integration

down into the heat where imperfection
unfolds into its potential—Ah!
The entanglement.
Is this where we finally wake up?

. . . .

flashes & dots & pings & ticks &
dots & lines & circles & waves & …
no, not yet—*if the moon is there*
why are we not compelled to look back?

We are existence after all, are we not?

Ah, to fall in love with that act
of observation (whether it was
actually there)—no, not in the polarized
light hanging over the city. Yes—,

we *are* entangled you & I—

what one does the other sees,
what one sees the other does,
the other sees what one does,
the other does what one sees—

SIBYL'S *CHANSONS DE LA BELLE ÉPOQUE*

(i)

Clear your mind
of dreams, she says.
Don't wander
into the night, but
into the heart
of sunlight
among the
vanishing shadows.

(ii)

Mirage, she says,
is in the doing,
not in the having
done; the workday
is a damp cloth
spun upon
the servile,
the slavish—

(iii)

Be aware of the clip
slip or knot
that holds back
progress.
Backcomb, she says.

(iv)

Then, a grimace, a smile,
a twist of the lips:
all-telling, she says.
It may become apparent
there is no such thing as delusion:
simply our chansons,
our two-part harmony.

(v)

& yes, the singer
is a winged creature,
a swooping crooner
of rhymes, a chanteuse
of lullabies & swansongs.

What of it?

TIMEBOMB

How we yearn for a vision, how we long
to cast a shadow
in a warrior's whirlwind.

Are you that man
beside the statue? she asks me.
In your pores, in your blemishes,
detail blurs … a broken vessel—
then, the dazzle
of a single chromosome
which for sooth
cannot be seen, vanishes:
for it is too small
to cast a shadow
& remote as distant suns.

Yes, infinity lurches away
even when we believe
we've come within line of sight.

Where is the epicenter
within barefooted experience
& all those conceptual riddles?

Only our probability remains, but
so much more delicate,
the fugitives, so much more
startling than the robust dogma
of this sky darkening above.

Still, she says, consider the silence.
It wavers, falling in hesitation like snowflakes,
landing here & there & there.

SIGH

Do you recall
the weeds dancing
in their late-summer orgy
or the wanton
applause of flowers opening?

& that sluggard sun
milking the stream
of your body
all the way through
the slush
of late autumn?

I forget …

I brace the wind
& this rumor
of your passing
carries me away.

You know,
in the very end
each poem
summer breathes
into me
empties me
of myself.

III. THE SLUMBER

Underneath the Arch of Constantine a swarthy sibyl slumbers.
When she awakes the gate will crumble.

—Gerard de Nerval, trans. Robert Bly

Decomposed into splinters of sayings,
We are a grave of words
Feigning language
To help us rummage through the everyday.

—Erika Burkart
(from "Speak and Hush," trans. Marc Vincenz)

OBLITERATING KNOWLEDGE

Uncle Fernando considers his homeward journey

Was he taking revenge
on reality? pointing out
flaws in order to mock
birdsong, foliage, or those
flamboyant Tuscan castles
slumping upon hills
that broke the light
in turrets & moats &
crumbling arrow-holes?
Could war be beautiful?
he asked himself.
Could love be more
than the sum
of human failings? & when
streams converge into rivers,
when the herons wander
beyond marshes
to root out worms
or other senseless
burrowing things—or,
the slug, a spoof
of a creature with its virtue
of snot that serves
no admirable purpose
grazing its way
through our roughage—
Was it only in the flowering
of his own fingertips & woes?—
no, not in the suffrage itself,
but in the dross of lament & tears,
in the unfinished

buildings that lined
his perfectly conceived
cityscape drawing him
into the middle of
absolutely nowhere?

BURNING THROUGH PAPERWORK

Eyeing everything that hampers progress—
a progress that once informed you
when you were sixteen,

poised hell-bent at arm's length
from your mother's sunbed tan,
she whose fingered lip

insisted on total silence
after 8:00 a.m.—
(she wanted to hear pins dropping

through the morning)
for that other man
who warmed her bed,

who worked the long dark hours
of a Scottish coal miner,
who rose at one to prepare them

in rouge & lipstick.
& with his sticky comb
for the dead, he always said

flour & water
was the best grouting
for a dead man's acne scars

& so he hauled
his bodies home in the back
of his shocking blue Rover,

two by two, working through the night
& into dawn, turning deathly white
into rosy memories

for the faithful & assembled,
etched & hued in his handmade caravan,
a contraption that carried a sweet-

bitter fragrance which was the iron tang
of bourbon infused with embalming fluid
in equal measures & just a hint

of Trident peppermint gum ...
"Lights out," mother sighed
drawing curtains on the sky outside—

just as now you too are considering
turning daylight into night,
& night into an eternity

of smooth cookie dough
for a new assembly-line girl who needs
to keep her mouth tightly zipped, but then

a mute swan sings
a last heavenly dirge
at Apollo's shiny feet.

STURM UND DRANG

After we rambled
from Chamonix
to Mont Blanc,

pausing once or twice
at wayward inns
to drink stale tankards

of Swiss ale
which quickened
the spirits, we

spied canals
on the moon
& faces on Mars.

What a paradox!
Uncle Fernando has said,
that species are so immutable,

so alike in design, yet
so changeable
in their devilish details—

& within the whorl
of the wave, the language, the culture,
the news: invention assuaged—

& when all the foolish wit
& whim was dusted off,
the living world

was so demonstrably different,
the polar reverse:
a right-hand-left-hand physiology—

in just a handful of amino acids
expelled in a burst of gas
from the guts of the Earth.

WHEN UNCLE FERNANDO CONJURES UP
A DEAD-BIRD THEORY OF EVERYTHING

CHAPTER FOUR
*In Which Our Dead Bird Seems to Come to a
Forgone Conclusion*

Out in the confines of time, space
or anything else, just try to find me ...

but what when we (are) no longer matter?
moving into the shadows of the impossible?

Does the participator create the new world?

In the words of the oracle, freeing up a multi-
verse of parallel (even conjoined) outcomes,

splitting history like cells in their probable variables.
What are we aware of then, my sibylline love?

Are we nothing more than weavers or craftsmen?

fine-tuners of simple patterns?—&, the question,
can our patterns be arranged in sensible ideas?

Who has the tools to tell the whole suburban story?
Please elucidate: What do you think then is this primal urge?

Not to forage or hunt, but to know the unknowable?

SPIRITS OF THE STONE AGE APPLAUD
THE REEMERGENCE OF DANCE

(i) Sibyl in Calabria

Stonecrushed & starstruck,
her villanelle eyes—
what fancy footwork
along these fair-weathered planks!

Between sharp shoes,
an ankle strap, toe-heel-toe
her taffeta & russet ruffle,
the crackle-snap of *Do-si-dos*,

of silk under hand-held fans,
he leads her back, back
through heaves & sighs,
through breathy chuckles

& fingered thighs, through
the boisterous & monocled,
the crumpled & vitrified,
or those certifiably certified,

burning hard-won earfuls—
he leads her through ruffians
scraping for copper coins &
their how's-your-fathers

standing tall, past the retired
brigadier tossing a rose or
three condescending army majors
ironed & greased in poker palms—

until the bellow & guffaw is hushed
by flowing velvet drapery,
by the promise of lace finery, of garters
behind a haven of plate-spinners,

of fire-jugglers, of torso-bending girls—
& other delightful balancing acts
where the rumble of rope on steel
clears the air for more barrel-tumblers,

for vague depictions of Buffalo Bill
where the Wild West plucks banjo
& the *How* of Sitting Bull
is the how-now of blue blood—

(ii) Drumroll

But wait!

Here's that potbellied
porkpie-hat man
in his flaming red blazer
fingering his rim & whistling

through his podgy fingers …
& sometimes
(but not tonight)
he whips out his tiger-tamer

in an pale offering
of supple pale skins
between shins,
between twirling ankles:

"Let us welcome them one & all,
Gentlemen, Laggards & Spiders!
Tonight we have not twelve,
but fourteen Little Miss Muffetts.

"So peel back your eyes, gents!
& peel your fingers for the house.
Look for the diamond in the fishnet.
No, no, this is not titillating Toulouse,
or the Grande Dame of Montparnasse
with her indulgent perfumes.

"Tonight you find your burlesque surprise
in decadent Callabria!—Bottoms up boys
& here's to the goose & not the gander!"

(iii) Les Fantastiques

& the cheers resound
in cacophony & the barks,
& the rumble & hiss
of those who lost it all once again,

pickled on il Vino Valente,
sozzled on Absinthe, or, in fact,
the Colonel who prefers
his Gins bright pink—

to ease their troubled souls
& whisper sweet-nothings
to the leg-tossing cancan girls
on their once-in-a-lifetime tour of Italy:

"Les Fantastiques!"

& in amongst the motley, watch for:

Signore Vesuvio
Professore Giovanni Melliore
Alberto Malcontento

&, look! & here's

Mister Reginald Smythe in from Tyneside
for a week of haggling Milanese textiles—
he who owns a bespoke tailorshop
in Knightsbridge, now nibbles breadsticks

& there's Great-uncle Fernando, dapper
in his spats even if he's just off the boat—
he slipped in on the sly,
he with the constellation of Libra

accompanying him even this far from Jakarta.
& then there's Il Gran Dottore—
less monogrammed, more hen-
pecked, tapping his pockets, playing

the loose change of gallstones
& munificent births
& that single death, not of his eldest,
but a frail boy with tuberculosis

who coughed himself
into the deepest sleep of all.
"Hey up!" yells Dottore.
"Hey up, girls!"

(iv) Prima Ballerina Assoluta

So what's a middle-aged man to do
but enjoy these rubbery delights
early on a Sunday morning
long before sunrise, or—

but who is she, the third from the right?
She with the red hair in the shadows,
she with the turnout like a danseuse.
Is she the sweet waltz of sirens?—

Unwinding his pocket watch to check
the time on his mind, it occurs that:

Fortune favors the bold.
Fortune favors the wicked
& sometimes
fortune favors the blind.

UNCLE FERNANDO'S ADVICE
ON CHASING THE FLAME

Let us be scattered wild,
let us be free as weeds—
for are we not just the size we see?
& at the bend ahead, understand
it is neither curve nor crossing.
Yes—let us not know
what we are thinking,
for in truth we really don't want to—

But isn't it a day of perfect light?
& for God's sake, don't ask questions like:
Does nature have an inside?
Even if you surmise that all
will dematerialize in a wing beat,
you can still eat an apple
& know its true meaning.

& why your childhood is a blur,
why reality has no use for you.
You watch everyone converge
on a line just out of reach, asking
if they are all they suppose, asking
if they have good reason for tears,
thinking they might catch clouds
or goad motes from under the bed.

Let us lean toward the infinite with the sense
      that somehow we lean toward ourselves
& let us preserve the flame that each night
      may buzz in the memory of a sundrenched day,
so we might know what it means to be truly sad,
      to be truly simple,
to be calm as trees.

A BRISTLECONE PINE
MAKES FOR NO MAN'S LAND

In summer's
heat, one thousand
flourish, yet

no *one* divines
success's
truest measure.

Standing apart,
billowing as
a mighty general

red-veined
in autumnal days, thin-haired
in wisps of grey

she leads
the final charge
straight over the top.

A FULL MOON OF CAPITAL ASSETS

Down where boxes are folded not only
to contain the thanks of every new born,
but also the regressed-back-into-childhood, third

from left, a Korean man-child with rosy cheeks
throws you a grimace as if he's had it right up to here …
He wants to bark *sorely underpaid*, packs sugar-
bricks to build an army of the super-fed.

He wants to clench, squeeze & twist,
toss you with all his heft against a wall
filled-in with calendars of runway models

& sporty girls in training bras, wants you
to haunt these halls long after cardboard
& crumbs, flickering in strip lights, nights
converted into a parking lot suspending cars

from steel frames, tracks for needy commuters
you just can't leave to their tawdry devices.
No such thing as fair distribution, he thinks.

&, who does stand up to a relentless capital mind?

Venus emerged resplendent from an oyster
on the half-shell, but what soul
wants to dwell forever in exile, watching
a tide rise & fall from the sidelines?

SIBYL'S VAGARIES OF TIME

My prison cell—my fortress …
                                    —Kafka

(i) In the name of commerce

We descended into the flame
          where ash was strewn

high as citadel walls
          to hold in all we held

esteemed, guarded
          the gilded & the burnished,

those enviable treasures
          that sang to us in our sleep

less siren, more in step—
          a rhythm we had become

accustomed to—it was then
          he handed me that chalice,

simple in craftsmanship
          without adornment, brimming

in blood-hot wine,
          made, he said, with tough

fingers of the toughest
          souls & steeped in vagaries

of old, to nourish us
          upon our lonesome journey

deep into the complex heart
      of simple things.

      (ii) Sibyl was her name

She who gripped my hand
      who walked with me in time

to the soothing song
      that occupied my waking

dream—in her flowing robes
      a magical vision who might talk

to Christ—drew me into the copper
      light of the flame, as the wine

burned on my tongue;
      all of this she said

in the name of a king,
      a word she tucked

fiercely in her breast
      when she suckled

me to sleep.

      (iii) & into the wheel

The sky grinding
      the chaff of the universe,

or the waterwheel returning
      life back to the face

& then, the early machines
      tapping power everywhere

& all the busy progeny,
      the draft animals

in their yolks & chains,
      harnessed to increase

the surplus—at least,
      this is what she said …

But who am I to know
      what from what,

in that strange becoming
      which is your other

mind becoming.

(iv) Panhandler in the Present Tense

She grunts upon reaching
      the summit—a sigh

of relief perhaps?
      or perhaps her way

of saying don't-forsake-me-
  God-in-the-next-fifty-six-steps—

weary eyes betray the rest,
  yet, yet, (what a frazzled fringe you have).

Did she have God
  in her pocket like the pearl I held

in my jimmy sack?—
  along with those three nuggets

(alack! alack!) of triple sec gold;
  why the fundament plays

beneath our feet;
  I wonder if she might

decipher love as I do?
  with destiny in her ear?

"What do you know of destiny
  with all that gold

in your jimmy sack?"
  She knows only steep hills,

inclement views, burdens
  of a make-believe love,

& then, as we move down-
  slope, something extraordinary.

She bats her eyelashes,
    carelessly leans into the air, & says:

"How many wild asses
    does it take to fall in love?"

(v) Absolute Hunger

We scrounge the data-
bases, but imagine
a scourge

stamped out
until you are
no more

than flat pieces
of your own self-
replicated eight—

(a penny halved
on a railroad track)
to become untraceable

when even that loon's
eye is sealed tight,
& the credit cards

expired—
        I know
you named

your fate
        long ago
& what you came up with
        was worse
           than you'd read:

to have starved
half-to-death
in someone else's home
        movie.

Now the moving eye
        roves again
by that medicine

in the garbage bag
with that megaphone
made of a Coca-Cola can.

The question is:
Can you really trust
your senses?

    (vi) Meta-

physical
morphosis
'nalysis
…
data
ringing
in your ears,

someone
tapping
a keyboard
in vain,

in your name,
not in God's.

SIBYL'S IMPECCABLE SENSE OF TIMING

Assuage   assign   assay
the asymmetry of our

Dead Sea Scrolls
don't be contented

in the suffrage
of the saline

or that streamline
of an enviable script—

      (the hand flowing
      fingertip-lit

      feathering the roughshod
      into delicate intricacy

      no bulb fizzling
      in phosphor, no camphor-

      sticks jostling
      in shrinkwrap

      not a semblance crackling
      in religious authenticity)

neither you nor I
in eyelock hovering
over fishstew

Come about   come astern

steaming hot
on hot-cold

The wave, the rush—
Just think
candleflame

flickering between us
like the stammering
of summer

or that kernel
of imperceptible
truths—

so sanguine
so simple
so supine

WHEN UNCLE FERNANDO CONJURES UP
A DEAD-BIRD THEORY OF EVERYTHING

CHAPTER FIVE
In Which Our Dead Bird Realizes that Religion is a
Form of Cryptology

A botox paradox, & once again,
looking for a missive or message
in the plurality of motions, in the shifting skies
in the stratosphere of oceans—

even in skintone & the amniotic shift

of textile on firm skin, to simplify
the ordering of sensory experiences—
order needs to emerge even when
it emerges somewhere else.

Reality must exist, surely, even

if nature itself depends on its perceptions.
So tell me now, as you empty
your last glass, tell me
of that great all-encompassing metaphor.

What disquietude we possess as we dive

into the unknown on a hero's journey
in our limitless desire to become something
of everything, not just a dot or a wave
watching constellations rise &

spin on in unspeakable desires—

is this the true measure of bliss?
beast nudging beast?
Let me hand you these fragments
of a bygone era that they may deliver you safely

into the bruised heart of a promised land.

IV. SIBYLLINE

Not odd that what's on my mind,
when expressed, comes out weird, jumbled. Don't berate;
no gun with its barrel screwy can shoot straight.
*   Giovanni, come agitate*
for my pride, my poor dead art! I don't belong!
Who's a painter? Me? No way! They've got me wrong.

—from *The Complete Poems of Michelangelo*
(trans. John Frederick Nims)

175

THE MERMAID & THE MONKEY

i. An unsurpassed rule of thumb:

Opposable.
Approachable.
A parable.

Unprecedented.
Percentages.
Patronage is a political strategy.

Perspective revolutionizes everything we see.
It touches the skies

& casts its shadow over distances,
over the humors of a city.

• • •

In the next great commission
it's the taste that matters—

glorifying the original sins
of the *maestro della bottega.*

& the birth of Venus,
Botticelli's pagan mythologies—

to stop the devil dancing
on his shoulders,

that master of misogyny.

177

ii. & to measure the light in all things,

to see Daniel in the lion's den,
serene rather than heroic

(in motion)
& the projection of human form
on heaven's body,

just as Apollo became Jesus
& the blue light
in an Attic August surpasses

the details of posture &
the colonnades & the columns &—

   • • •

a natural selection of forms feeding

on the spiritual crises,
on the human,
on the heroic,
on the divine,

from within the vault of dark ages
which follow the Fall

   • • •

& into the hands of dictatorships,
despotisms or democracies

& other magical words that rattle
in the spiritual comfort of relics,

in the concrete substance
that civilizes—

where the true nature
of a building

is forgone space.

       • • •

& the dreaming magi
in the vaults' echoes

in the love's labors of citizens

giving way to the splendor

of the city giving way
to the flocking pilgrims

or the "effects of good governance"

that surpass
the Black Death

      iii. & the Greatest city of Rome in decay in a day,

the outpouring
where Death itself

becomes a public theater—
in suspension …

Where God made man
because he loved to hear stories—

Christ's agonies for woman & man
in a time when there was no divorce

& the scales of Archangel Michael glimmer gold

as armies march on
to bombard city walls,

& then that falling
upon Aladdin's den
as Christ upon his cave

     • • •

& the four horsemen
rhapsodic,

tantalized by tortoiseshell
& rhino-horn & quetzal-feather

as surmised in Dürer's *Ritter, Tod und Teufel*—

melancholy on the dark side of genius

& that last word.

     • • •

The Teutonic torture—
the twisted hands of the virgin;

O, the therapy of music
in the Atomic Age

& the torment & trial in the wilderness
the wild fantasies of Grünewald.

Was Aztec gold
a vision of the future?

  iv. & in the Pantheon where Rafael was buried,

The Transfiguration,

a measured symmetry
of high society, unfinished.

The Last Supper, a ghost.
compelling, yet

lascivious, licentious
&—elusive.

In completion, reduction
or transfiguration.

The dichotomy of Apollonian or Dionysian principles.

& then, the self-doubt
of an artist with a heroic ambition.

& from that Goliath of marble
the small block of David
from the very skin of the stone,

an evocation
to impress
all comers.

• • •

Watch!

As Plato points
toward heaven
Aristotle points
toward the dirt.

& as God touches the finger of Adam,
so Adam touches the hand of another—

so tantalizingly tender
that spiral upon spiral

in the spirit
of the index finger.

v. & all this unity, wisdom, wealth &, an ideal projection

The illusion of two canopies.

Surely there's more to this canonization lark?

Even when Mercury, our god of money,
gives the party an elevated status

among the doctors & the magi,

how to remain
        at the center
                of power

& rework
        the word
                of love?

        vi. Loft & air

No brush, no chisel
lightens the soul.

To work though stone,
to find the wall of love

& the ice—
the wall of ice

now dissolves
in unison

with the industry of men,
rhetoric, theater & illusion—

to dramatize yourself
as an ideal man,

rich in trade & craft
& so to come to some fortuitous conclusion

behind the mask
of democracy

in this Pantheon of small gods,
& the desire

to impress

Minerva,
       Mercury,
              Apollo.

Unique in the world
of ever-blooming Myrtle.

       vii. Light through glass in the Annunciation

YHWH.

The lion, the divine love.

Spaces of unpredicted clarity;
the turbulent light
that emerges
through the darkness.

Across the altar
              in the mass
as the glory
            of angels
suffuses in light.

& in the down-glow,
dogs play
just enough

to convince us
to believe.

THE INFANT & THE STINGING NETTLE

i. Counterrevolution

The seeing & adorning,
& where the mind will be
taken care of,

in the harmony
of the spaces
loved in, lived in.

From this place
the water services

the kitchens, the gardens
& the most excellent fruit.

This painting is large
& could hold

many many
figurines.

ii. The eyes that behold

in the fountain of the aristocrat's garden
among the swans & ducks,
& goldfish,
the king of the beasts
brandishes a sword—

& once again
the light resounds
divine providence

& the bees carry
the keys to the kingdom.

Is it not a time
to draw perspective?

iii. The heartbeat of a building

Transverberation.

Fragrant hymns of praise
& divine celebration—
the smoke of creation.

Journeys that do not end.

Surpassing the sweetness of pain,
the institution's divine right to rule.

What is the vocabulary of power?

You can't read the features
until you're up close to the travails,
observe the naked benevolence,

the descent from the cross
with only one hand
on the reins—

• • •

O the arcs & the swirls …

Where the eye cannot focus
as one myth assails another

& suffused with nostalgia
within the shadows
of sculpted space,

in the everyman
of everyday
departing for the Isle of Cythera.

iv. & in the microcosm of the garden,

the effects of past time,
the truth unveiled,

movements
between the hills & the dales.

• • •

The art of liberty.

The staking out of order
& that fever
of Revolution.

Was it just the failure
of the harvest?

or was it the oath
in the mausoleum?

v. A secular coup d'état, *a political ideal*

Now the stars of the empire

    far from the magic bean

        of enlightenment,

the urban proletariat

    & the clouds of Revolution

        gathering.

The abstraction

    that prepares us

        to give our lives.

The anecdotal.

    A natural being

        with untamed appetite.

The primacy

    of the eye

on the surface of appearances

An imprecise definition of form.

O how the light

modifies matter

& toys with grand design.

vi. Worshipping the serene Buddha

When does the disquiet
become bourgeois

& the yawning background

descend

in celestial revelations?

v. On the Sun's consciousness

How to handle the modern?
How to find a kiss
for the whole world?

Behind a beautiful curtain
the objects of mystery & desire.

The dislocation.

& the savage made congenial through—

impromptu, flimsy,

but deadly serious
pure plastic rhythm.

•   •   •

O to follow the flight of the swallow
through the storm of the future

& to become
that bird
in space
in your own right.

vi. How to remove the object from the center of the eye?

Space & sense

       & the dream

& then, the enthusiasm

of Man as iceberg.

All those babblers, dilettantes & swindlers

opening doors

into different futures,

following the minotaur.

    vii. But a shadow falls upon history

repairing the shattered cultures
& thus
backs
turn

into their own expression
followed by sand

& waste

& rubble,

o—no subject,
but content …

no document
seared
in the corners

of a lifetime
within a fixed timeline
degrading the colors—

      •   •   •

the speed of change,

    the saturation

        of objects,

            packing,

preparing

    for a wide spread—

    •   •   •

unheroic,

anywhere,

anything,

no more windows,
but a field, a horizon,
an assemblage,
a tremulous clutter

in the small,

the mundane,

the profane, then the real

viii. & the disposable,

A libation.
A liberation.

The transformation of the flesh,
sweeping away,
generating a vision
of what already is

with immediate
content—the dissidents
& their images of glory.

Watch closely!

• • •

Here come the corporate collectors.

Abstractions have become ordinary
& the myth of progress
grinds down to a tiretrack.

What controversy?

ix. Where's the leverage in the pluralism?

What then can we say
of the symbols of belief?

Can you hear the silence
of history breaking?

The phantoms inform
but do not transform.

•   •   •

Inject yourself back
into the earth
& become a sphere.

Become evidence
of former lives.

You can only predict
the probability
at odds
with experience.

x. Still, in the knot of perspective,

a voiceover says:

All roads are travelled.
Vibration determines everything.

O, if only
for a quick, tight
Hollywood
ending.

NOTES AND ACKNOWLEDGEMENTS

"Listen" is for Robert Bly.

"Circling the Polestar an Empty Mind Mirrors the World—" is for the Chinese Tang Dynasty (618–907) poet Li Po (also known as Li Bai, Li Pai, Li T'ai-po, and Li T'ai-pai).

"*Homo Erectus*: Cinnabar": Cinnabar has been mined far back in man's history, both for its red color as a pigment, and later for its mercury content. Cinnabar came to be known as vermillion and was used by painters during the Renaissance and for coloring laquerware in ancient China. Pliny the Elder, the Roman natural philosopher, stated that no other commodity was more carefully guarded.

"Song of Enchantment" is for David Sylvian and Thomas Feiner.

"As Cold and Passionate as the Dawn" is after W.B. Yeats and alludes to the Hermetic Order of the Golden Dawn, the organization that Samuel Liddell MacGregor Mathers founded (1887), and which included Yeats and Alistair Crowley among its early members. The title comes from the last two lines of Yeats' poem, "The Fisherman."

"Vision of Cave Fire" is after the bison painted on the cave ceiling, Altamira, Spain. Many of these cave paintings were executed over 35,000 years ago.

"The Saturated Brilliance of the Queen of the Night" is for and inspired by Alexander Dumas' novel *The Black Tulip*.

"Seeking a Pregnant Emptiness on the Banks of the River Po" is for and inspired by the Tang Dynasty Chinese poet Wang Wei, a great master of the jueju form.

"Aphrodite and the Flood" is for and inspired by Pompeo Batoni (1708–1787), an Italian painter known for his allegorical and mythological paintings.

"Prometheus's Spotted Liver": As a punishment for giving humanity the gift of fire, Zeus had Prometheus chained to a pillar and sent an eagle to consume his liver during the day. Every succeeding night Prometheus's liver was restored again. For the Romantics, Prometheus was the rebel who resisted all forms of institutional tyranny. As stated by Franz Kafka, "The legend [of Prometheus] tried to explain the inexplicable. As it came out of a substratum of truth it had in turn to end in the inexplicable." (trans. Willa and Edwin Muir)

"In the Penal Colony" (*In der Strafkolonie*) is after Franz Kafka's short story of almost the same name (first published in October 1919) and for Dante and his own inferno.

"Skypointers and Gunclimbers" is after Marsden Hartley.

"In the Magnitude of Errors" is after the Roman philosopher-poet Heraclitus (approx. 535–475 BCE), known for his insistence on continual and ever-present change as being the fundamental essence of the universe.

"Ode to a Metalworker in the Sumerian Heaven" is for the Swiss philosopher, physician, scientist, alchemist and astrologer, Paracelsus (Philippus Aureolus Theophrastus Bombastus von Hohenheim) (1493–1541). He was a contemporary of Copernicus and Leonardo da Vinci. Ko Hung was a Chinese philosopher, alchemist and prolific writer during the Jin Dynasty (265–420).

"Uncle Fernando's Advice on Chasing the Flame" is after, and inspired by, the Portuguese poet Fernando Pessoa and his many alter egos. Pessoa's imaginary personas held many conflicting views. By the end of his career he had written under more then seventy heteronyms. According to Pessoa, his main three heteronyms were Álvaro de Campos, Alberto Caeiro and Ricardo Reis. These heteronyms possessed very distinct personalities, temperaments, writing styles and philosophies. Several of them were in serious conflict with Pessoa himself.

My thanks are given to the editors of the following publications, where these poems (and in some cases earlier versions) previously appeared:

Ploughshares
The Nation
Raritan
Notre Dame Review
New American Writing
The Common
Solstice
diode
decomP
The Manhattan Review
Public Pool
Hinchas de Poesia
Plume Poetry
Plume Anthologies 3, 4, 5 and 6
Plume Interviews 1
Ragazine
Ocean State Review
spoKe Journal
Unlikely Stories Mark 5
Fulcrum
Truck
The Journal of Poetics Research
World Literature Today
3:AM Magazine

"Sibylline" was previously published as a limited-edition chapbook, illustrated by Louisiana artist Dennis Paul Williams (Ampersand Books, 2015).

ABOUT THE AUTHOR

Born in Hong Kong, MARC VINCENZ is British-Swiss and is the author of ten books of poetry; his latest are *Becoming the Sound of Bees* and *The Syndicate of Water & Light*. His novella, *Three Taos of T'ao, or How to Catch a White Elephant* was released by Spuyten Duyvil. He is the translator of many German-, French-, and Romanian-language poets. His latest work of translation, *Unexpected Development* (White Pine Press, 2018), by prize-winning Swiss novelist, poet and playwright Klaus Merz, was a finalist for the 2105 Cliff Becker Book Prize in Translation. His work has received fellowships and grants from the Swiss Arts Council, the Literary Colloquium Berlin, the National Endowment for the Arts, and the Witter Bynner Foundation for Poetry. His own recent publications include *The Nation, Ploughshares, The Common, Solstice, Raritan, Notre Dame Review, New American Writing, Los Angeles Review of Books* and *World Literature Today*. He is International Editor of *Plume*, publisher and editor of MadHat Press and Plume Editions, and lives and writes in Western Massachusetts.

For the full Dos Madres Press catalog:
www.dosmadres.com